# Betsy's Birthday

Peter Bently

Illustrated by

*Emily Fox*

**OXFORD**
UNIVERSITY PRESS

# OXFORD
## UNIVERSITY PRESS

Great Clarendon Street, Oxford, OX2 6DP,
United Kingdom

Oxford University Press is a department of the University of Oxford.
It furthers the University's objective of excellence in research, scholarship,
and education by publishing worldwide. Oxford is a registered trade mark of
Oxford University Press in the UK and in certain other countries

Text © Peter Bently 2017

Illustrations © Emily Fox 2017

The moral rights of the author have been asserted

First published 2017

British Library Cataloguing in Publication Data
Data available

978-0-19-837728-3

3 5 7 9 10 8 6 4 2

Paper used in the production of this book is a natural, recyclable product
made from wood grown in sustainable forests. The manufacturing process
conforms to the environmental regulations of the country of origin.

Printed in China by Leo Paper Products Ltd.

**Acknowledgements**
Inside cover notes written by Becca Heddle
Author photograph by the Fatherhood Institute

# Contents

# Chapter 1
# An Early Start

Betsy the bushbaby woke up and
blinked in the afternoon sunlight.
Bushbabies are normally asleep all
day and awake at night. But Betsy
was excited. Only one day to go
until her birthday! And there was
something else as well.

"Now, what was it?" Betsy thought. "It was to do with Dad … Oh, I remember!"

Betsy trotted along the branch to Mum and Dad's bedroom. They were still fast asleep. But not for long.

"Wake up, Dad!" cried Betsy. She bounced up and down on Dad's chest.

Dad grunted sleepily.

"Go and get that big lion!" cheered Betsy. "You sort him out! Hooray for Dad!"

Dad opened one eye.

"What *are* you going on about, Betsy?" he muttered. "What big lion?"

"The one you're going to fight," smiled Betsy. "I can't wait!"

"WHAT?" Dad sat upright. He was wide awake now.

"Mum told me about it," said Betsy cheerily.

Now Mum sat up.
"WHAT?" she said.

"You said Dad wanted to fight a big lion today," said Betsy. "Remember?"

Dad stared at Mum.

"What, me? A *bushbaby*?" he spluttered. "Fight a *lion*? Are you crazy?"

"Oh, *Betsy*," sighed Mum. "I didn't say Dad wanted to FIGHT A BIG LION. I said Dad wanted QUITE A BIG LIE-IN!"

"Oh, *Betsy*!" moaned Dad. "I was looking forward to a nice long snooze!"

"Oops," said Betsy. "Sorry, Dad. Sorry, Mum."

"You *must* listen more carefully," said Mum. "You're always in a daydream!"

After some tasty figs and eggs for breakfast, Betsy wanted to go out to play.

"Hold on, Betsy," said Mum. "Can you get me some things while you're out?"

Betsy wasn't listening. She had seen her friend Freya the flamingo, who was flying over the tree.

"Oh, yes, Mum," Betsy said dreamily.
"I'd love to get you some *wings*. It would
be fab to fly, wouldn't it?"

"Betsy!" said Mum. "Stop
daydreaming. I said I need some
THINGS, not WINGS."

"Sorry," said Betsy brightly.
"What do you want me to get?"

"Some figs for tonight," said Mum. "And some reeds for a mat. The mat in our bedroom is worn out. Got that, Betsy?"

Betsy nodded. But she was thinking, "If *I* had wings I could fly over the forest and visit all my friends!"

"One more thing, Betsy," said Dad. "Can you pick a pear for Aunt Nina? It's her favourite fruit. She's in bed with a cold. I'm popping over to see her later."

"Sure, Dad," Betsy nodded. But she was thinking, "If *I* were a flamingo I could sleep standing on one leg!"

"Now, off you go," said Mum. "We'll have lunch just after dark. Make sure you're back in time!"

"OK, Mum," said Betsy. But she was thinking, "Yes, being a flamingo would be *such* great fun!"

# Chapter 2
# Muddy Muddle

Betsy clambered down the tree and headed along the forest path. She saw Freya the flamingo in a pond.

"Hi Betsy," said Freya. "Where are you going?"

"Hi Freya!" said Betsy, as she walked past. "I have to do some chores for Mum and Dad. I need to— Wow! That's amazing!"

A big green lizard was scurrying along a nearby rock.

"Watch out!" said Freya. "There's a hole in the path!"

But Betsy wasn't listening. She was too busy looking up at the lizard on the rock.

"I've never seen such a fast lizard!" said Betsy dreamily. "I wonder where it's going?"

"Mind where you're walking, Betsy!" called Freya. "I can see a hole in the path! Are you listening?"

"What? Of course I'm listening," said Betsy, still following the lizard on the rock.

"You said you can see a mole in the bath … EEK!"

Too late. Betsy tumbled head first into a muddy hole. Freya went over to help her out.

"Bother!" Betsy said crossly. "Freya, why didn't you warn me, instead of going on about a mole having a bath?"

"Oh, Betsy!" chuckled Freya. "I said I could see a HOLE IN THE PATH, not a MOLE IN THE BATH. But you weren't listening properly – as usual!"

"Oh. Sorry," mumbled Betsy, wiping the mud off her face. "By the way, will you come to my birthday party tomorrow?"

"I'd love to," said Freya. "I'll bring you a present. What would you like?"

"Oh, I don't mind," said Betsy. "A new ball?"

"Sure," said Freya. "What time is the party?"

"Seven o'clock in the evening," said Betsy. "I hope that's not too late for you. It's *early* for bushbabies. We're up all night and sleep all day."

"That's fine," said Freya, flying off home. "See you tomorrow!"

Betsy carried on along the path. Then she remembered her chores for Mum and Dad.

"Now then," Betsy thought. "What was the first thing Mum asked me do? Give someone a BIG FRIGHT? ... Or ... get some WIGS that are WHITE?"

A gust of wind sent a large leaf fluttering past. Betsy watched it float and dance on the breeze.

"It looks just like a kite!" she thought.
Then she cried out. "*Whoops!*"

She had tripped over a twig lying on the path.

"Of course!" she said gleefully. "Mum wants some TWIGS for a KITE. She must be making me a kite for my birthday. Well, that's easy. There are plenty of twigs lying around."

# Chapter 3
# Banana Drama

Betsy soon found one long twig and one short one. She picked both of them up.

"Yo, Betsy!" said a squeaky voice behind her.

"Eek!" Betsy jumped with fright. She whirled around to see a meerkat popping out of its hole. It was her friend, Mia.

Mia said,

"What are you going to *fix* with those two *sticks*?"

Mia liked to speak in rhyme.

"They're for a kite," laughed Betsy.

The meerkat grinned.

"A *kite* in *flight*

is *quite* a *sight*!"

"Are you coming to my party tomorrow?" said Betsy.

Mia frowned.

"Sorry *dude*,

I don't want to sound *rude*,

But the party's not too late, I *hope*?

If it's past my bedtime I'll have to say *nope*!"

"Don't worry," said Betsy. "The party is at seven o'clock."

Mia was delighted.

"Way-hay! *Hurray!*
You won't keep me *away!*"

"Great!" said Betsy. "I'd better go. I have some more things to— Hey! Look at those termites!"

Under a clump of trees, a long line of termites were marching in and out of their tall nest. Betsy went over for a closer look.

Mia tried to stop her.
"Betsy, don't go that way, *please*!
The chimps are playing tricks in
the *trees*!"

"Hmm?" said Betsy as she wandered
under the trees. But she wasn't really
listening. She was daydreaming about
the termites. "It must be incredible to be
so small!" she thought.

Mia cried,
"Betsy, keep *clear*!
Didn't you *hear*?"

"Oh yes," said Betsy dreamily.
"You said I'll glimpse some baby
chicks eating peas. Don't worry, I
won't disturb them."

Mia squealed in alarm.
"Betsy, *wait*!
Oh no, too *late*!"
PLOP!
SPLAT!
SPLOP!
Three stinky rotten bananas landed
on Betsy's head, one after another.

"Ugh!" Betsy yelped. In a tree above her, some cheeky chimps were giggling.

"Whoops-a-daisy!" said the first chimp.

"Hee-hee! I dropped it by accident, honest!" said a second.

"It just — hoo-hoo-hoo! — slipped out of my hand!" said a third.

Mia chuckled, wrinkling her nose.

"Betsy, I tried to *tell you*, and now I can really *smell you*. Pooh! I said the CHIMPS are PLAYING TRICKS in the TREES, not you'll GLIMPSE some BABY CHICKS eating PEAS! You didn't listen."

"Oh," Betsy said. She scraped the bananas off her head. "Anyway, I'll see you at my party tomorrow."

Mia nodded.

"I'll bring you a *gift*,
if you get my *drift*.
What shall I *bring*?
Some creeper for a *swing*?"

"Thanks," said Betsy. "But I'd really like … a pirate mask!"

Mia said,

"I'll do my *best*.

Now, I'm off to my *nest*

for a bit of a *rest*!"

Mia popped back into her hole and Betsy wandered on down the path. She was careful to walk *around* the clump of trees.

# Chapter 4
# Splash Dash

It was now early evening.

"It's getting dark," Betsy thought. "I'll have to go home for lunch soon. What was the other thing Mum asked me to get?"

Betsy was so busy thinking that she bumped into her friend Emlyn the elephant. He was on his way to the river for a drink.

"Oof! Sorry, Emlyn!" said Betsy.

"Daydreaming again, Betsy?" said Emlyn. "I nearly squashed you flat!"

"I'm trying to remember something," said Betsy.

"I think I have to get some CHEESE for a CAT. Or … something to FEED a BAT?"

"And *I* think you haven't been listening, as usual!" chuckled Emlyn. He looked at the sky. It was full of dark clouds. "Yikes! There's a storm on the way!"

"What?" said Betsy, who was only half-listening. "Oh no! Argh! Help!"

She dropped everything, ran to the river – and jumped in the water!

"Betsy! What's the matter?" cried Emlyn. He fished her out of the river and plonked her on the bank.

"You said there's a swarm on the way!" said Betsy, dripping. "I hope it's not a swarm of wasps. A wasp stung me once. It really hurt!"

Emlyn trumpeted with laughter. The tears rolled down his trunk.

"Oh, Betsy!" he giggled. "I said there's a STORM on the way, not a SWARM. You weren't listening, were you?"

Betsy looked embarrassed.

"Anyway," she muttered. "Are you coming to my birthday party tomorrow? It's at seven o'clock."

"I'll be there," said Emlyn. "Elephants never forget! I'll bring you a present. What would you like?"

"That's kind of you," said Betsy. "I'd really like … a dinosaur!"

"OK!" said Emlyn. "I'll see you tomorrow!"

Emlyn was right about the storm. It soon started to rain. All around, animals ran for shelter.

Betsy jumped out of the way as a family of shrews scampered for their burrow, holding leaves over their heads.

"That's it!" Betsy said. "Mum wants me to get some LEAVES for a HAT! She needs something to keep off the rain."

# Chapter 5
# Hyena Hullaballoo

As soon as the storm stopped, Betsy gathered some leaves. She tucked them under her arm with the two twigs and headed back home.

"Hold on," she said. "I'm sure *Dad* asked me to do something, too. Was it STICK some HAIR on a LEMUR?"

"There aren't any lemurs around here," said a gloomy voice. It was Harry the hyena and his twin sister Hetty.

Most hyenas like to laugh. But not Harry and Hetty. They never laughed. They were the gloomiest hyenas in the jungle.

Suddenly, Betsy remembered what Dad had asked her to do. She trotted up to Harry and Hetty – and poked them in the ribs.

"Ooh! Ah! That tickles! He-he-he-he!" Harry squawked.

"Ha-ha-ha! Ho-ho-ho-ho!" chortled Hetty.

Betsy prodded Harry and Hetty until they were rolling on the ground in fits of laughter.

"He-he-he! Oh, it's good to laugh again!" guffawed Harry.

"Ha-ha-ha! Thanks, Betsy!" tittered Hetty.

"My pleasure!" grinned Betsy. "See you later!"

Betsy headed for home. She scrambled up the tree into the nest.

"Hello, Betsy!" said Mum. "Did you get the things I asked for?"

"Oh yes," said Betsy.

She placed the twigs and the leaves on the table. "Some TWIGS for a KITE, and some LEAVES for a HAT. Just like you asked!"

Mum's eyes opened wide.

"Oh, *Betsy*!" she sighed. "I wanted some FIGS for TONIGHT, not TWIGS for a KITE. I was going to make us a fig pie. And I asked for REEDS for a MAT, not LEAVES for a HAT! Betsy, you *really* must listen more carefully!"

"Oops. Sorry," said Betsy.

Just then, Dad came in.

"Hello, Betsy!" he said. "What a racket those two hyenas are making! Why are they laughing?"

Betsy smiled.

"I did what you asked me to do," she said. "It worked!"

"Eh?" said Dad. "What do you mean?"

"You told me to give the pair of them a tickle, remember?" said Betsy.

Dad looked puzzled. Then it dawned on him.

"Oh, *Betsy*!" he sighed. "I said PICK a PEAR for AUNT NINA, not TICKLE a PAIR of HYENAS! When *will* you learn to listen properly?"

# Chapter 6
# Birthday Tricks

The next day, Betsy was very excited about her birthday. At seven o'clock, everything was ready for the party.

Freya was first to arrive.

"Happy birthday, Betsy!" she said. "Here's your present!"

"Thanks, Freya!" said Betsy. "I'm looking forward to playing with my new ball!"

But the present wasn't a ball. It was a large blue cloth.

"A NEW BALL?" said Freya. "I thought you said a BLUE SHAWL! I didn't listen properly. Sorry!"

Betsy didn't want to sound rude.

"Thank you," she said. "It's ... a very nice shawl."

Mia scurried out of the bushes.

"Happy birthday, dear *friend*! May your fun never *end*!"

She handed Betsy a present.

"Thanks, Mia!" said Betsy, tearing at the wrapping. "Now we can all play at pirates!"

Betsy opened the present and saw the face of a brightly coloured bird.

"Oh! Did you want a PIRATE mask?" said Mia. "I thought you said a PARROT mask. Sorry, Betsy! I wasn't listening properly."

Betsy was disappointed, but tried to hide it.

"Thanks," she said. "It's ... a very funny mask."

Finally, Emlyn arrived.

"Happy birthday, Betsy!" he said. "Here's your present. It's just the right size for a bushbaby!"

Betsy unwrapped Emlyn's packet to find a very small tool for cutting wood.

"You did ask for a TINY SAW, didn't you?" said Emlyn.

"No, a DINOSAUR," said Betsy. "But thanks. It's very ... *useful.*"

Betsy wanted to sound grateful. But she really *didn't* like her presents.

She looked at her friends. They were trying not to laugh. This was too much.

"What's so funny?" Betsy burst out. "*None* of you gave me what I asked for. If only you'd all *listened* properly!"

"We're sorry, Betsy," smiled Freya. "It can be a pain when someone doesn't listen, can't it?"

Betsy opened her mouth to answer.
Then she realized what Freya had said.

"No. It's *me* who should say sorry,"
Betsy sighed. "Everyone is always telling
*me* I don't listen properly. Now I see how
annoying that is. In future, I'm going to
listen more carefully."

Mia whooped with delight
"Woo-hoo! *Way-hay*!
Our trick worked *today*!"
"Trick? What trick?" said Betsy.

"We wanted you to know what it feels like when people don't listen," said Freya.

"So we pretended to get the wrong presents," chuckled Emlyn.

"*Pretended?*" said Betsy.

Betsy's mum and dad appeared, carrying a large box.

"Ta-*daa!*" said Mum. "Here you are, Betsy. Happy birthday from all of us!"

Betsy opened the box. Inside she found a new ball, a pirate mask, a toy dinosaur – and more presents besides!

"We *were* listening really!" said Freya.

"That's brilliant!" said Betsy. "I'm sorry I got cross. Thanks, everyone!"

"Right," said Dad. "Let's get on with the party. I've made a big CAKE!"

"Eek! A big SNAKE? Where?" cried Betsy. Everyone stared at her. Then she laughed. "Only joking! So, who wants cake?"

## About the author

I live a long way from the jungle in the cool town of Totnes in South Devon. I have written lots of picture books, including *Cats Ahoy!* (which won the Roald Dahl Funny Prize in 2011), as well as the *Knightmare!* young fiction series. *Betsy's Birthday* is inspired by my daughter Tara. One night, when she was about four, we were all really tired. I told Tara that Mummy and Daddy were hoping to get a *lie-in* in the morning. The next day, Tara was very disappointed when she realized we weren't actually planning a trip to Paignton Zoo to bring home her very own pet *lion*!